Foreign Wife Elegy

POEMS BY

Yuko Taniguchi

COFFEE HOUSE PRESS

2004

Coffee House Press books are available to the trade through our primary distributor, Consortium Book Sales & Distribution, 1045 Westgate Drive, Saint Paul, MN 55114. For personal orders, catalogs, or other information, write to: Coffee House Press, 27 North Fourth Street, Suite 400, Minneapolis, MN 55401.

Coffee House Press is a nonprofit literary publishing house. Support from private foundations, corporate giving programs, government programs, and generous individuals help make the publication of our books possible. We gratefully acknowledge their support in detail in the back of this book.

LIBRARY OF CONGRESS CIP INFORMATION

Taniguchi, Yuko
Foreign wife elegy : poems / by Yuko Taniguchi.
p. cm.
ISBN 978-1-56689-148-6 (alk. paper)
1. Japanese American women — Poetry.
2. Hiroshima-shi (Japan) — History — Bombardment, 1945 — Poetry.
I. Title.

PS3620.A685F67 2004
811'.6—DC21
2003055095

3   4   5   6   7   8   9

This reprint has received special project support from the
Archie D. and Bertha H. Walker Foundation.

PRINTED IN THE UNITED STATES

ACKNOWLEDGMENTS

I am truly grateful for the guidance and support that Michael Dennis Browne, Ray Gonzalez, and Jim Moore have shared with me. Thanks to Kathleen Glasgow, Elizabeth Noll, Michael Seward, Michelle Matthees, Sister Mara Faulkner, and Sister Eva Hooker for their support and for providing literary community. I wish to express gratitude to Jennifer Pecore for her hard work and to all of my family members who live all over the world, but somehow always managed to touch my life.

Good books are brewing at coffeehousepress.org

for Peter

Contents

1

11 Foreign Wife Elegy

12 Blue Eyes

13 Promise

14 Susan

15 Kathleen

16 His Day

17 Winter Race

18 Kiss

19 Small Disasters

20 After Working at the Hospital

21 Ocean

22 He Said

23 Foreign Words

24 Elegy with Music

25 Foreign Wife

26 Our Day

2

29 Grandmother's Mouth

30 Dying for Flowers

31 Red Sweater

32 Mother's Camellia

33 Ice Fishing

34 Mud Shoes

35 Traveling Rock

36 Waiting

37 New Year's Day

38 Another War

39 My Father

3

43 Name

44 Talking to Myself

45 Ichirou

46 Practice

48 Gold Hair

49 Henry the Handsome Fifth

50 Sam

52 Beating

53 Colony

54 Yellow Poems

56 Dark Room

57 Turning

4

61 Under the Sun

62 Scratching

63 Ingrown Toenail

64 Earthquake

65 Rain Dance

66 Feeding Birds

67 Lonely Week

70 *Elegy for Cello and Orchestra* by John Williams

71 Human Noises

73 In the Middle Seat

74 Breathing

75 Soliloquy

76 Stillness

77 Going Home

78 Poem

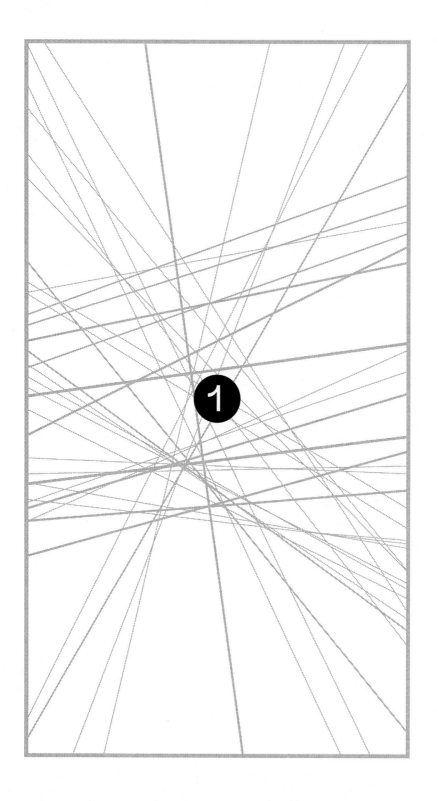

Foreign Wife Elegy

My language has its own world
where he doesn't know how to live,
but he should learn my language;
then he can call my mother to say
that I am dead. I drive too fast
and someone else drives too fast
and we crash on the icy road.
The death sweeps me away.
He can tell this to my mother
if he learns my language.
Her large yellow voice travels
and hits his body, but at least she knows
that I am dead, and if I die,
I want him to tell my mother
with his deep voice shaking.

Blue Eyes

I used to believe that people with blue
eyes saw everything in blue.
In summer, I longed to see

in blue like living underwater.
I dropped my eyes into a blue bottle
and asked my husband to carry it around.

Every day, he worked at the hospital; all the buildings
seemed colder. When his eyes peeped in the bottle,
I saw the well of tears moving behind his eyes.

When I woke up, it was already autumn.
All day, I gazed at my husband, busy
collecting red and yellow leaves in our yard.

Promise

On Highway 55, Mr. Hartman's brain crashed hard into
the windshield the way we crash open an egg.

By the time doctors sewed back his bones and skin, all
the water leaked from the well of kindness in his head.

Since then, he cries and screams in a voice he never
had before. He moves violently, like a blinded horse.

Once, my husband pinned Mr. Hartman's strong body
down on the hospital bed, and medicine splashed

from the arm tube into his blue eyes. After washing his eyes and
testing his blood in the emergency room, he came home

with red eyes. If I suddenly become a different person
instead of death, promise to leave me, he said.

Over and over, he made me promise to leave him.
At night, I lay next to him and listened to the water moving

behind his face. His well is always full. Water moves with
time; when it passes us, we have no way of gathering it again.

Susan

All day at the hospital, my husband cleaned the countless open sores on Susan's body, her skin curled up like a dried rose. Almost none remained. No one knew why her body began to tear itself up. He cleaned each sore gently, though she thought he was stabbing her. That night, she dreamed of her body turning into liquid all at once, like ice cream left in the sun. That's how fast I want to go, she told him, as fast as I can melt.

Kathleen

Because Kathleen was young and healthy, because she was a mother and a wife, because she didn't mean to die, but was willing to bleed and tolerate the sharp pain in her liver, because it was not a mistake when she swallowed fifty grams of Tylenol, because what she did surprised her and unfolded the path of death in front of her white toes, my husband tried to save her, even after her liver failed. Nothing stopped the bleeding from her eyes, nose, mouth, and anus. The complex living that continued on and on was suddenly ending. *What have I done?* all night, she mumbled.

After Kathleen's death, my husband sat still like a white rose on a thin, straight stem. What holds the layers of rose petals together is not strength, but a fragile hope that grows on and on out of nothing, and eventually becomes tears in the center of a stem.

His Day

In the early morning, my husband gets dressed in dark blue scrubs at home. At the hospital, Mrs. Johnson, in pain, holds her faint breath. He fixes a clear tube that trembles on her neck. Mrs. Baker's skull was cut open for twelve hours last night to scrape out all the bad cells. A silver needle sits on Mrs. Miller's arm; her ripened skin swallows morphine, melting her eyes. Mrs. Morgan spills applesauce on her shadow. She cries for her nurse.

At noon, his stomach is full of hospital air. He washes his hands and closes his eyes for a moment.

In the afternoon, Mrs. Carlson breathes too fast in her sleep. He leaves nitroglycerine under her tongue, burning wood in her mouth. Later, when she wakes up, he listens to her story: "My husband was strong, but he never brought Jesus home." He opens her Bible and smells the old afternoon. He reads her Jesus and tucks her into the bed.

At night, he comes home and I hold him. We listen to the water boiling for our ginger tea. I kiss his chapped hands; love feels like ginger in me.

Winter Race

From the tenth floor I.C.U. down
to the exit door, a nurse ran out late at night
to the local restaurant for a small container of tomato sauce,
then ran back, white air coming out of his nose like smoke.
He pushed the entrance door, leaving his fingerprints,
back in the elevator to the tenth floor,
to room #1003 for the woman without her kidneys,
liver, and half a stomach. She wanted to taste
tomato sauce one more time.
Her gray lips parted, like a pair of rusted scissors.
He fed her with his chest moving up and down, breathing fast.
His skin, iced outside, melted as if his whole body were in tears.

Kiss

Jack was only five years old when his mother's heart stopped beating. He sobbed, shook her and called her name, but when nothing awoke her, he kissed her forehead. Hours later when my husband cleaned her body, her forehead had a small wet circle. He washed her face carefully around Jack's kiss.

Small Disasters

I poured a glass of water, ran downstairs to do laundry, and hours later, felt thirsty. My water was warm, sitting patiently on the table. Think one thing at a time, my husband says. But which thought should I think? I feel lonely, want to see the ocean again, cut my nails, buy more milk, remember my dream from last night while I forget to drink the water. All the things I neglect return to me as small disasters. All day long, water dripped from the faucet.

After Working at the Hospital

deep in the night
               he follows a long
gray road. in the ditch, he stops
               to empty his stomach.
his shoulders shake,
               but he is invisible.

deep in the night
               he touches my hair.
he washed a dying woman's
               hair, yellow and soft
like overcooked noodles,
               which absorbed all
the rain on earth.
               deep in the night,
my hair disappears.

Ocean

Late afternoon, we argued
with many words randomly crossing
between us. We couldn't swallow
any of them.

We sat silent on the shore and watched the ocean become
invisible at night; the sound of waves reverberated
and slowly accumulated inside us. We listened until
the waves became a form of forgiveness, intangible,
endless.

He Said

He said he has never seen the ocean;
he has never smelled the salt
that wakes him inside. He has
never fought against the water that pulls
his feet back to the center of earth.
He has never drowned, or felt the soft
water covering his mouth, the sound
of waves echoing from the inside
of his body.

He has never seen the ocean.
Where does he let his memories sleep?
If he drowns, who will come and find him?

Foreign Words

When my husband pronounces *lovely* and *scary*
in Japanese, they sound the same: *Kawaii* and *Kowai.*

To match the sounds, meanings, and intention,
he practices speaking alone—*lovely, lovely, lovely.*

His familiar words are across the ocean, though for the deepest
sorrow, the death of our friend, our mouths become dry.

No words match our intention.

Elegy with Music

after Prélude Suite No. 1 in G Major *by Johann Sebastian Bach*
Unaccompanied Cello by Yo-Yo Ma

When Mr. Kokai died, I was in the airplane, thinking about how
everything resembles something.

A rose resembles layers of time.

June resembles blue eyes.

A river resembles forgetfulness.

The sound of Bach resembles certainty.

Certainty resembles the thin balance of regret and hope.

Death resembles a long night and peace.

Elegy resembles prélude.

When Mr. Kokai died, I was in the airplane, thinking that he was
going to die soon. I was no different
from those who cried listening to Bach years ago,
those who lived urgently, those who died, those
who live to die.

Foreign Wife

My husband asked me where I would go if he dies.
Foreign wives are homeless without their husbands.
We give up our homes at the wedding.

So where do foreign wives go after the death of their husbands?

I would walk into our bedroom. The smell of his presence has no
name, but its warmth would remind me that I am not alone, that I am
alone. No one would know that I was sitting on our bed.

Our Day

On Sunday afternoon, spring has come,
although it is February.
I ask you to lie down next to me.

By tomorrow, you have to review the heart block,
how *P* leads to *QRS*
and to *T* on the electrocardiogram,
and I have to write how my hand curled
like a dry leaf in your hand this morning.

I ask you to sleep away the afternoon
with me, even though we have all this work
and no time to close our eyes.
Spring arrived too soon today;
I want you to lie down.

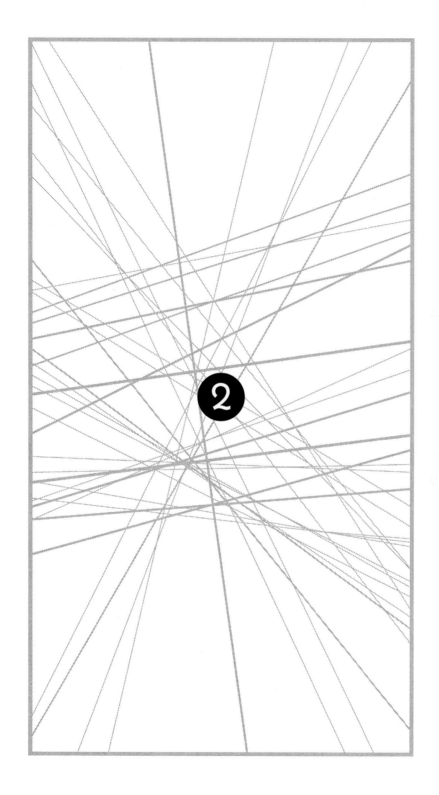

Grandmother's Mouth

My grandmother's teeth grind rice
and pickled daikon. Soon, the white
is reduced to pulp in her saliva,
thick like glue, full of small bubbles.
I want her to swallow the juice,
but she keeps chewing
the shapeless food with wet sound.
This is how she has lived.
She beats everything
until nothing functions
any longer; her children.
Why has no one taught her
to swallow before the food loses its taste?
If she could taste the sweetness,
she would know the simple
answer to her life.

Dying for Flowers

Don't die, little flower.
I'll die instead.
—ANNA SWIR

My mother used to say flowers are better
than children; we don't always return
what we have received.
My mother carries heavy pots every morning
from our dark house to the outside.
Under the sun, she cleans the dust off the leaves
and touches each flower tenderly
with both hands. If she could touch me like that,
I would die for the flowers.
My mother should always have many beautiful
flowers growing around her.

Red Sweater

I bought a red sweater for mother
to hide the ribs
pushing out of her skin
creased to hold her barren body.

I saw her once
wearing my red
and bony smile, stealing
my eyes.

Our love is rusted
iron sinking deep
in ice.

Mother's Camellia

The Camellia holds layers of pink petals.
Human eyes can hardly believe this delicate
arrangement. At the end of spring, the Camellia
falls suddenly from its neck and hits the ground
like the beautiful head of Macbeth.

Ice Fishing

On the frozen lake, Dad makes a hole with a large silver
stick. We stand on the bright snow. I could squeeze

my body through this hole like a snake. I want to
see the other side of the closed earth, but the water would

sting my body with its sharp needles. I was not made
to see every side of the earth. I hook a small fish

attached to a clear line, to a rod, and to my hand;
we control everything here.

Dad says a fish's mouth does not feel pain when it
swallows the hook. He says this because I am only

six years old. I prepare a guest room for the fish:
a blue bucket from the car. When my line is pulled,

I reel in hard. I want to show this fish the bright side
of the earth: a green-and-yellow dotted fish in my hand.

His mouth opens, closes, opens, closes, drops
blood on the snow. I watch his black eyes turning pink

slowly out here on the bright side of the earth.

Mud Shoes

When I couldn't finish a bowl of brown rice, my father
told me to think of the farmers who wake up before sunrise,

work all day, and return home with mud shoes.
They work hard to feed all the children like me;

so be grateful, my father said. I forced myself to pack more
brown rice in my stomach. It tasted like those farmers'

sweat and mud. Once, I didn't finish my lunch. I threw
away the leftover brown rice on the way home from school.

That night, many mud shoes came after me in my sleep.
"I am sorry to be so ungrateful," I told them as I ran away.

But they passed me and went to the field.
I watched them get muddier, stepping hard on the ground;

the wet voice of soil lingered in the air.
In my pajamas and bare feet, I walked with them.

Traveling Rock

after the oil painting Rock Forms,
by B.J.O. Nordfeldt, Weisman Art Museum

Our mother's cheek almost fell off when her angry blood got stuck under an old tooth in the back. I thought a ghost was pulling her triangle cheeks. My brother and I took her to the dentist before anyone was awake, even the Sun. She lay on the black plastic chair, her mouth wide open, her shoulder trembled, shook the earth. We cried because she cried from the silver hook fishing in her mouth. Next to our mother, we prayed: *wind, come wind come, sweep our mother's tooth away, away to the south, east, north, and west, do not come back to us.* Then the power of the wind arrived: her tooth, a bloody rock with gray and green spots, fell out. I put it in a small box and ran to the ocean. By the shore, I threw it and prayed: *sweep our mother's tooth away, away to the south, east, north, and west, do not come back to us.* Twelve years later, I found his portrait in Minnesota; he had arrived in California from the Chigasaki shore. He heard my prayer. He sits lonely by the shore of California, away from our mother's mouth.

Waiting

When I was ten, my brother went out in the rain
during a stormy night to swim in the ocean.
In my dream, I wait for him to come back
even though he safely returned years ago.
My small body stands against
the ocean, glares at the violent waves, and waits
and waits for him to swim back to shore.
In my sleep, I wait for my brother.

New Year's Day

On the phone,
my father's voice
arrived a second
later, like an echo.
A thin wire ran between
us. I told my father
not to move. Do not
disturb the wire
pulled under
the ocean for
thousands of miles.
The distance between us
grows emptily inside me.
This terrible space is all
I have today.

Another War

From Yokosuka Base, American jets cut through the sky like silver shears across blue cloth. Every summer, foreign soldiers practice how to fly above my house. Windows shake. Trees sway. Our voices disappear into the sound of tearing sky.

This year, my father is fifty-eight years old. On his fourth birthday, burned trees rolled down the street in Hiroshima, and he ran to the river. Later, he grew up in the city of ash and learned to be kind.

He says we are fortunate to live in peace today. I don't sleep with my shoes on or dig ground for the air-raid shelter. But once, a man pushed me into his car; since then, every shadow is too close to me when I walk alone at night; since then, I run to the river like my father.

My Father

I asked my father what he will do
if I die before he dies.
He will stand, thank others
who loved me, and bury me
as soon as possible. Everything
will happen quickly if I die
before my father.
Only after he cleans
my room full of finger
prints, he will open
his dark mouth to call
my name. Like cursing,
he will call my name.

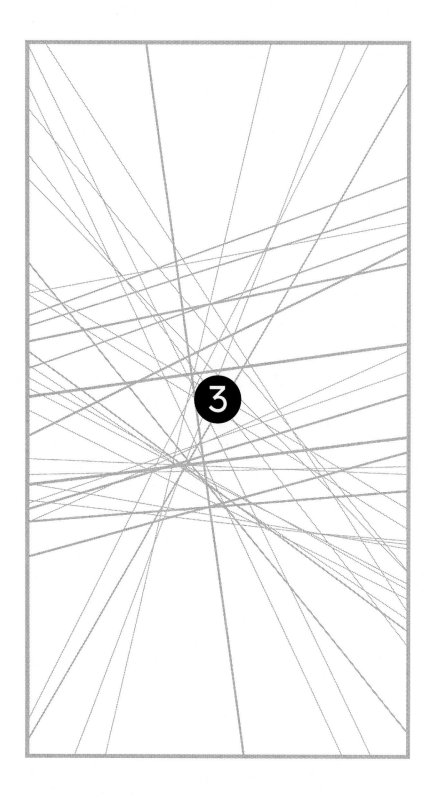

Name

You say my name
happens too quickly,
that it is difficult to
pronounce Yuko.

It is Yuko, like *you,*
and add *ko* at the end:
I spell it for you to see
the sound.

A sound is invisible.
You must cross the bridge
with your eyes closed
to touch my name.

Talking to Myself

Yesterday I wrote a poem about my mother's face.
She was disappointed, which curved deep wrinkles on her skin.

This morning, I felt the soft texture of her face in my hand.
She was laughing and singing in my dream.

My poem was no longer true.
She does not read English; if she could,

my poem would weave inside her chest;
she would suffer from my words.

She should never read my poems; I was just talking
to myself. I was talking to myself alone.

Ichirou

When Ichirou played *Prélude in A Minor* by Johann Sebastian Bach,
he saw the face of Bach above the piano, shedding tears like rain

on a mountain. Ichirou was a genius. We grew up together.
His hands were always restless, and he walked unevenly.

When he was fifteen, he stabbed his fingers with a knife
and left our town. Even now, his young hands still bleed

in my mind. Something had hurt him endlessly,
so he followed the river on the mountain that continued

all the way up to the sky. His grown hands no longer play
Prélude in A Minor. The rain falls on the mountain, exactly

and faithfully like the painful sound of Johann Sebastian Bach.
Ichirou has learned to hold the water with both hands.

Practice

But trust the hours. Haven't they
carried you everywhere, up to now?
—GALWAY KINNELL

I.

I practice piano and repeat scales one hundred
times every day because what we do today
becomes tomorrow's harvest; practice makes perfect.
Bach's prelude drops layers of voice all at once.
Over and over, I practice until I realize that the sound
full of sorrow demands a complete
separation from the pianist
full of sorrow.

II.

Walking into the dark tunnel alone
at night frightens you, though you may
overcome this fear if you practice
this every day, or you may never
overcome it like the terrible emptiness
inside you; it does not make you stronger.

III.

All the living that you did
suddenly seems like practice
for dying, but living is not supposed to be
a rehearsal for death. We are never ready
for departure, but the curtain is wide open
with lights shining on the stage. You are getting up
slowly. Soon you will walk away from us
as if to practice walking
for the first time.

Gold Hair

At the bakery, I cut a slice of vanilla
cheesecake for a young Asian man
with golden hair. His face stood
loudly in front of me.
We had the same face. *Is this how I look?*
I gave him the cake, and his sunflower
eyes curved.

He left the store as if to enter the forest
wearing bright hunting clothes.

Henry the Handsome Fifth

gently appears in my dream.
I take his lips as bees sting my skin, as butter
melts on croissants. His soldier's hand softly
touches the red curls covering my face.
My French breaks the silence, asking him to take me,
take a princess, take my love.
Yet he tells me my fashion of singing
my love is too loud and brave.
He, along with my red curls and French, disappears.
I am left alone with my face, suddenly Eastern
as if two scones were hidden beneath my cheeks.

I often forget my own face here.
This plain face is made of brown rice;
it tastes like water, yet feels sticky and thick.

Sam

day 1

Since Sam has arrived in our home, he has been hiding under the couch. His tail shakes out of fear. He wants to be alone, protected in a dark small space. But at night when the entire house becomes dark, his space disappears into one large blackness. Sam knows how small he is in this world. He cries by the door all night. Soon, the morning will come, and he will forget about his small life burning under the couch.

day 2

While I write poems this morning, Sam chews my colorful slippers under the desk. They bewitch his eyes. The sensation of his teeth pressing my feet through soft cloth pressures me to be serious about writing. I write as hard as I can.

day 3

After my husband leaves for work tonight, Sam is restless. He walks around the house. He already recognizes what is missing from the house. Knowing what we cannot forget is only the first step. Attachment is a terrible seed to eat. This seed will grow into a large emptiness. I have no wisdom for him; no one has overcome this lesson of love.

the end of the first week

In the middle of the night, the sound of Sam's footsteps and breathing comes close to my face, but Sam isn't here. The wind blows rain against my window. I go downstairs to see him sleeping peacefully. He has made peace with every noise that paralyzed him. He has opened his gate to this world. When he gets hurt, it will surprise him as if he has never felt pain before.

Beating

I raised my fist to him. What are you waiting for? He looked away. I shook my head and said it was too late. My fist, a burning rock above his head, was enough for him to hear the sound of bone crushing bone. His whole body trembled. He daydreamed of falling from a cliff. After the sensation of ultimate fear, there was no more beating left for me to do.

.

Colony

While I worked on my garden,
because Sam chewed on some flowers,
not as a punishment, but for my convenience,
I tied his leash to a tree.
Sam sat still. Quietly and desperately wanting
to be near me again, he watched me move.

When I released him, hundreds of ants clung
to his belly, chest, and beneath his tail.
The swarm of ants crawled, stung his soft skin and left
bloody marks with their tiny needles.

I washed Sam with cold water. Drowning ants went
down into the sink. Sam's bloody stomach healed
in the evening, but a thousand ants came
back to me that night. They stung my skin
on my head between my hairs, took my shoes
and buried them like sowing seeds for the spring.

The next day, I woke up; I am no longer a benefactor, but a queen
for the ants who won't forget the face they saw as they drowned.

Yellow Poems

I have seen
yellow poems
float on
the river
under the sun-
light, turned
into pink. They
traveled miles
and miles and
eventually
sank down
to the bottom.

I have seen
yellow poems
pull my long
black hair
until we came to
the bridge
that crosses over
deep holes,
our memories,
so we simply
returned to where
we came from.

I have seen
yellow poems
multiply in

my mother's mouth,
mostly dark.
Gray teeth
stand like buildings,
a city full
of little angry
people.
I have seen
yellow poems
coming out
of my father's
breath. He says
nothing, but the
sound of yellow,
in and out of
his chest, pulls
out my tears.

I have seen
yellow poems
in a glass
pretending
to be soft
liquid. I drink
them to be
a poet
who has
something
yellow
to say.

Dark Room

This afternoon, fever stayed inside my chest like water
in a well. The outside was unusually bright and blue
for February. I closed my eyes. The brightness sat warm
behind my eyelids, and I fell asleep even though I didn't
mean to. When I woke up, I was buried in the dark room.
How long did I sleep? The sun shone to death and burned away.
My day passed like an empty train moving on time,
leaving me behind.

Turning

Our dreams have been assaulted
by a memory that will not
sleep.
—WILLIAM CARLOS WILLIAMS

I.

Leaving is only possible with the intention
    of returning; otherwise, the loss seems unbearable.
        We numb the memories of our old lands,
equivocate the voice of a child inside us calling, *where*
    is my mother, where
        is my father?

II.

In humid June, my young sister-in-law
    and I go for a walk on the gravel road.
        Black dogs come after us,
barking with deep red inside their mouths.
    Their sharp teeth deceive our eyes. We
        believe their power and anger, but are they afraid
of our voices?
    We make a detour of five miles, never turn
        around to face the dogs' yellow fear.

III.

In August, my young sister-in-law has a terrible headache
    during her older sister's wedding. She is pale as a river
        breaks, flooding her inside.

My husband walks on a busy street in a strange city to look
　　for some medicine for her. The young girl's suffering
　　　　and his compassion tangle into a rope, which pull him
far. Will he know when
　　to turn around? Or will he be lost
　　　　in his compassion, inside her river?

IV.

It is always the same dream. After a dinner of deep-fried oysters,
　　I wash rice bowls and round
　　　　dishes for my family. The kitchen is on fire
with the smell of grease and sweat.
　　I drain the oily water; my mother
　　　　washes soybeans behind me
by the ashen wall. I am no more
　　than this wooden bowl full of beans.
　　　　I don't turn around to see her wrinkled face.
The smell of grease pulls me
　　out of my dream. I stay awake for a long time
　　　　until my feet grow warm.

V.

When the rice paper falls in the pool, water
　　presses hard against the fibers that connect its life.
　　　　When it dries, its shape appears again with uneven
skin and wrinkles and scars from the violence of the water.
　　All the bones joined tighter
　　　　without a space for softness, like our memories.
Nothing will undo our old loving.

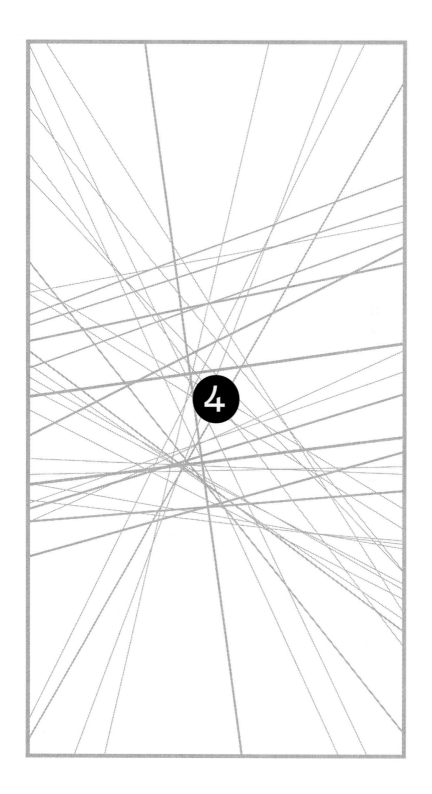

Under the Sun

The sun shines upon my back.
I hang wet clothes on the drying stand.
Soft warmth embraces my back, all the way
to my bones. For a moment, I mistakenly believed
that I was forgiven.

Scratching

I scratched my head according to the demand
of my skin's surface until blood stained my nails.
I didn't feel any stings. The sensation of relief and pain
remains close together, like the beauty of falling water
and the death that calls your name from the bottom
of the river.

Ingrown Toenail

I let my toenail grow
against me until the space
between flesh and skin
contains white blood. The nail
is determined to move on
regardless of all the body
in front, like plowing snow.
The nail doesn't recognize
his growth against his own kind.
I hesitate to interrupt him
for the sake of saving others.
How should I know who is more
worthy to live? He takes
another step. My skin screams.
I hear the fires. A young man lies
on the ground. I search for him,
thin, white, fully awake in the white
of my skin, and cut off his head.
Every war begins the same;
a few men choose who should die.
Such violence continues
and I will cut his head off again
and again. It won't take
long for my toe to heal,
but I must remember
how I fought against my own body.

Earthquake

Japan lies on the seam
where plates from the Philippines,
Asia, and the Pacific Ocean meet.
Each plate takes a step every day,
one tenth of an ant's step.
A tiny piece fell last night
under my grandmother's
house. I hesitate to call her
about her safety. It is not that I cannot
forgive her for all the lies, beating,
and hating that she did, but in the name
of love, I would speak kind words,
and she would know how hard I tried
and failed to love her. I am small,
standing on this wild earth.

Rain Dance

after Suite for Violin and Orchestra in A minor, Op. 10
by C. Sinding

Rain falls.
    Oval beads shatter flat
on my back; each powder of rain
    heaps to a drift of music.
I tie my black hair into one
    straight stream and run.
I run before my specific body
    scratches the shape of water.
I need to save this melody
    piling under the ground.
Someday, this music will break
    the links of dirt and stones
like the time my father was trapped
    in Kobe by a broken mirror
after the earth shook his building.
    I stood outside and asked forgiveness
for loving the harmony of rain
    that softened the ground like wet
newspaper losing its shape.
    But this summer, I see three sun-
flowers smiling with brown teeth.
    I am still in love
with the gathered sound of rain fragments
    melting into a lake.

Feeding Birds

I watch my husband walk to the empty
bird feeder. He holds his sister's small hand.
Seeds bounce on the glass from his hands.
From here, I want to touch his hair; it smells
like old wind. From here, I want to hold
his laughter flowing up into the white stream of sky.
From here, I want to cover his eyes before the dawn
shines on the snow. Winter, come close to me,
scrape my skin red. I will carry your sharp edge
before you sting his blue eyes.
I want him to come home soon.

Lonely Week

Rain

My father once told me
love is a glass, half
full of rain.

Circle

I am distracted
by the sound of the moon
rolling all over the sky
without leaving footsteps.

Ink

On your birthday card,
I write your name
in white ink. I trace
your name again and again
until the wet ink breaks
the paper. Then I know
you were here and passed me
without calling my name.

House

At work, I often wonder
if my yellow house
still exists; I have no
way of knowing this
until I return and see
my yellow house sitting
still, like an old man.

Sweet

A day after my birthday,
the sweet smell of strawberry
sauce stings my lungs.
I ate my cake alone at night.
my mother touched my neck
in the dream. My birthday
is her loneliness. I smelled
sweet strawberries in my sleep.

Yellow

I wash my clothes and fold them in perfect
squares in the morning. All afternoon,
I play the piano loudly. When I lie down alone
at night, a string of hair enters my mouth;
the foreign sensation alarms and
wakes me. The next day,
I am not ready for the sunlight,
spreading so much yellow.

Voice

My mother laughs in my dream. I laugh with her.
Our voices overlap and roll into our braided
hair. She is no longer lonely without me. I am
free to love her. This is all
I need to walk again.

Elegy for Cello and Orchestra by John Williams

It is a principle of music to repeat the theme . . .
until the thought is dissolved in tears.
—William Carlos Williams

Strings rub each other as his sorrow slips from the cello; he closes his eyes. The pain of *a* minor overflows from his fingers. He breathes in between *f* and *a*. Then *d* rushes into the stormy day, *e* breaks a berry on the falling night, *f* holds a dying light, *a* slides into a silver bowl, *d* erases a shadow with burning wood, *e* curves black night with silver rain.

Behind his eyes, where does the echo go? Behind my eyes, the echo takes me into the deepest part of the ocean. The ocean never moved until someone cried when she first breathed.

Human Noises

I.

Running in the morning, breathing
becomes a conscious choice to stay alive.
Once my body is used to
struggling, struggling
becomes normal again.
Running through maple trees,
my knees burn.

II.

Sam knows a stranger's footsteps from miles away.
He stares at black air, growls and barks at what he senses.
We lock the door. We have a gun. We don't sleep,
but no one breaks our door tonight.

III.

Since Mrs. Lee became a widow, she opens her window
and screams every night. She stares at the ground, considers
jumping out the window from the seventh floor.
He will never come home again.
As long as she stays alive, she is free
to consider death.

IV.

The way Sayaka moved to put on her coat brought the awful
sensation back again. The image of a man, his sweaty odor,
weight, and voice revisited her. She sat still, commanded
her lungs to breathe slowly, waited for the memory to
become vague in her body.

V.

The word "overcome" signifies
something to come toward us;
we are expected to walk over it without looking away.
True overcoming means to survive the random
sounds that we make: a man and a woman talking, boiling
    water, cutting
vegetables, windy night, a girl shouting, baking fish, ocean
    waves.

Between each noise, we eat, sleep, walk, notice, remember,
    endure, survive.

In the Middle Seat

A little boy is crying in the middle seat of the middle section in the airplane. *I want to sit by the window, I always see the sky, how come I can't sit by the window today?* His voice changes from whining to sharp yellow anger. His screams and cries overwhelm the closed space. His mother softly tells him that she will try to make things better. This is how a lie begins. Tell him the truth; this is only the beginning. He will be hurt again, but even in the darkest space of the middle seat, he must wait and hope out of disappointment.

Breathing

The way you breathe,
from your mouth to your lungs,
should be corrected,
a doctor once warned me.
Always close your mouth
and consciously breathe
from your nose, where
the small hairs prevent
bacteria from entering your body.
I teach my body how to breathe.
My nose does not swallow
enough air, which frightens me.
Suddenly, sleep seems dangerous.
I might choke myself to death, or, if
I open my mouth, bacteria will hurt me.
After learning to protect myself, there is nothing
I can do but to undo the protection.
Surviving requires a certain naiveté.
Even though it's risky, I open my mouth
and breathe with blind faith.

Soliloquy

after Soliloquy, *from* Sonata for Cello and Piano
by Athena Adamopoulos

The lake did not
protest when I
took a bucket of
water. All night,
the wind makes
the water sway
right and left.
They whisper
in a rustling voice.
Under the moon,
in the middle of
the forest, the lake
heals itself, forgetting
that I was there.

Stillness

after Red Violin *by John Corigliano*

They told me that the ship never came
    last night, but I thought I heard the water

being sliced. When something loose
    like water is cut, there is a smell of burned salt,

like the way a violin is cut by strings and
    bleeds out of fear and tenderness.

In the midst of this dark red,
    we become what the sound signifies.

Every motion cuts something, even this black ink;
    the remaining shape is the silence, stillness of our minds.

Going Home

My home is another village away.
How did I come here, sitting here, smelling the dust?
Grasses get stuck on my sweaty face. I stand in the vast
orange of the afternoon sun that covers me and I disappear.
This is a short trip home; each color tangles and finds me.
It wakes what has accumulated in me—blue
of the ocean, white from the moon, and the vast
orange that hasn't stopped dripping from the sun.

Poem

The wind swings
a leaf round
and round
in the air;
the sky drops
its vast blue
on the surface
of the ocean.
I listen to the old
sound, humanly
full and silent.

Poetry from Coffee House Press

That Kind of Sleep by Susan Atefat Peckham

it was today by Andrei Codrescu

A Handmade Museum by Brenda Coultas

Maraca: New and Selected Poems 1965–2000 by Victor Hernández Cruz

Routine Disruptions by Kenward Elmslie

The Cloud of Knowable Things by Elaine Equi

Red Suburb by Greg Hewett

*Notes on the Possibilities and Attractions of Existence:
Selected Poems 1965–2000* by Anselm Hollo

Legends from Camp by Lawson Fusao Inada

Teducation by Ted Joans

Gorgeous Chaos: New and Selected Poems 1965–2001 by Jack Marshall

You Never Know by Ron Padgett

Earliest Worlds by Eleni Sikelianos

Transcircularities: New and Selected Poems by Quincy Troupe

Breakers by Paul Violi

In the Room of Never Grieve: New and Selected Poems 1985–2003
by Anne Waldman

The Magic Whip by Wang Ping

The Annotated "Here" and Selected Poems by Marjorie Welish

Available at fine bookstores everywhere.

Coffee House Press is a nonprofit literary publisher
supported in part by the generosity of readers like you.
We hope the spirit of our books makes you seek out
and enjoy additional titles on our list.
For information on how you can help bring
great literature onto the page,
visit coffeehousepress.org.

FUNDER ACKNOWLEDGMENTS

Coffee House Press is an independent nonprofit literary publisher. Our books are made possible through the generous support of grants and gifts from many foundations, corporate giving programs, individuals, and through state and federal support. This project received major funding from the Jerome Foundation and the National Endowment for the Arts, a federal agency. Coffee House Press also received support from the Minnesota State Arts Board, through an appropriation by the Minnesota State Legislature; and from grants from the Buuck Family Foundation; the Bush Foundation; the Grotto Foundation; Lerner Family Foundation; the McKnight Foundation; the Outagamie Foundation; the law firm of Schwegman, Lundberg, Woessner & Kluth, P.A.; St. Paul Companies; Target, Marshall Field's, and Mervyn's with support from the Target Foundation; The Walker Foundation; West Group; the Woessner Freeman Foundation; and many individual donors.

This activity is made possible in part by a grant from the Minnesota State Arts Board, through an appropriation by the Minnesota State Legislature and a grant from the National Endowment for the Arts. 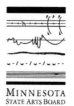 MINNESOTA STATE ARTS BOARD

 NATIONAL ENDOWMENT FOR THE ARTS

To you and our many readers across the country, we send our thanks for your continuing support.

Good books are brewing at coffeehousepress.org